Victorious Love

Victorious Love

THE PURSUIT OF A SPIRIT OF EXCELLENCE

BY JOHN EROL KOCER

FOREWORD BY
PASTOR LARRY BURD

TATE PUBLISHING & *Enterprises*

Published by Tate Publishing & Enterprises, LLC
127 E. Trade Center Terrace | Mustang, Oklahoma 73064 USA
1.888.361.9473 | www.tatepublishing.com

Tate Publishing is committed to excellence in the publishing industry. The company reflects the philosophy established by the founders, based on Psalms 68:11,

"The Lord gave the word and great was the company of those who published it."

Published in the United States of America

ISBN: 978-1-60247-527-4
1. Christian Living   2. Sipritual Growth: General

07.06.15

Foreword

John Erol Kocer reminds me of a gold miner. He has an unusual ability to study a passage of Scripture, discover nuggets of truth within the text, polish them and then present them in a profound, yet practical manner. That's what he has done with the Gospel of John.

In this book, *Victorious Love*, the author personifies Jesus Christ as the essence of victorious love. Love is victorious because Jesus Christ is victorious in all He does and says in the Word of God. Just as "God is love" even so Jesus is victorious love as demonstrated throughout the Gospel of John.

In this book, the author allows God to use his personality to communicate biblical truth in a fresh and exciting way. His use of rhyme is not distracting, but delightful. "Listen, Jesus left His glory to tell us His story. Bask in His presence and partake of His essence. Listen to His words, hear what He has to say, speak with love and authority to those who walk your way."

I have known John Erol Kocer for many years. I have had the privilege of being his pastor and have seen *Victorious Love* demonstrated in his life. I have a much deeper appreciation for the author as a man of God as a result of reading his book, *Victorious Love*.

I trust you will be a better "gold miner" and find many "nuggets of truth" as you read this book based on the Gospel of John.

Pastor Larry Burd
February 2007

Chapter 1

From the start of all time was Love, for our Father is unconditional love and all He has created is because of this love. (See John 1:1; 1 John 4:8, 16.)

Love, light and life are all synonymous as you cannot separate any of these wonderful facets.

Love is the most powerful force upon the face of this earth. It will penetrate all it comes in contact with.

Love unites, heals, sanctifies and sets us free from all activity that is not pleasing to our Father. He truly provides us with the most splendid victory.

As I study the Book of John, I continue to see our Father's love poured out upon all of His creation.

When John walked on this earth, his motives were questioned by some of the religious leaders. (See John 1:19–28.) Jesus always deals with the hearts of people. Religion tends to deal with the intellect which cannot comprehend the heart without a revelation from the all encompassing Spirit of God.

"…Behold the lamb of God, which taketh away the sin of the world." (John 1:29)

It is up to us to release all of the sins, past and present, so we can truly walk in our freedom.

Will you do this today? Allow the Spirit of Love to reveal all that needs to be cleansed. This way, we can take a more promising and powerful journey within His cleansing Spirit.

Will you also allow Love to purify your heart, mind, soul and body of all that contaminates so that He can provide the most accurate coordinates?

It certainly is time to walk the straight paths that have been set before us.

Will you fulfill the holy calling He has placed within your heart? Now is the time to start.

How! true

You cannot change the past but you can certainly learn from it. You will truly change your future by changing the present.

When Love extends His invitation to you and says "Come", will you bow from within and submit or will you continue to walk your own way?

It is time for the Body of Christ to be in harmony with the Head, Who obviously is Jesus.

Let's truly strive for excellence. It is so important to come up to a higher level and view the world as Jesus sees it. The earth is His but the world operates on a totally different playing field.

Chapter 2

Jesus is a man full of love and miracles.

Mary, the mother of Jesus, realized this as she spoke to the servants prior to the first miracle Jesus performed while walking on this earth.

"His mother saith unto the servants, Whatsoever he saith unto you, do it." (John 2:5)

Are we willing to do the same? Will we do whatever Love tells us to do?

"If ye be willing and obedient, ye shall eat the good of the land." (Isaiah 1:19)

Love always provides His best as is evidenced by the performance of His first miracle of turning the water into wine. (See John 2:7–11.)

Allow our Father to do His best for you by communing with Him on a daily basis.

Submit, commit and emit Love's very essence by spending time in his presence.

Allow Him to reveal His glory so that your faith can grow. How can you trust someone you do not know?

The world will demand that you show them outward appearances as they rely on the physical senses. We however are to voice "…the truth in love…" (Ephesians 4:15)

Do our words penetrate the hearts of people or are we actively involved in debates? Do we even share His heart with others?

Will we enter our Father's best provisions of abundance and blessings? If so, we need to communicate with Love Himself, allowing His power and force to set us free from all captivity.

> The Spirit of the LORD is upon me, because He hath anointed me to preach the gospel to the poor; he hath sent me to heal the broken-hearted, to preach deliverance to the captives, and recovering of sight to the blind, to set at liberty them that are bruised, to preach the acceptable year of the LORD.
>
> Luke 4:18–19

Whoever you are in your journey today, please remember that the God of all miracles is waiting to show Himself in the most powerful way.

If you will study the whole creative process of the

force of Love, you will truly realize that it could and can only be done from the One above.

It is glorious to partake of His goodness. For in Him, you will truly experience Love's richness.

Yes, many will believe when you share His heart with others, and miracles will follow that could be done by no other.

Please stop concentrating on doctrinal differences for this only produces strife. Be led by His ways which always produces life.

Chapter 3

Jesus said "…Except a man be born again, he cannot see the kingdom of God." (John 3:3)

Of course, religion immediately questions the validity of this statement. Why? Because the natural person is always trying to reason within himself. Christianity is not a matter of the intellect but a reflection of a heart to heart connection with the God of all creation.

You must be born of the Spirit of the most high God if you ever want to enter heaven. This is in reference to the scripture noted above.

It is a matter of faith or trusting in His compassion, love, mercy and goodness, as a beautiful place has already been prepared for you. This place is inconceivable by our own natural ways of thinking. Jesus says "Come and see all that I have for you. Trust Me, trust Me, for I will lead you in the paths of life."

Please stop looking in the natural, for true changes must first take place within your heart.

When you become born again, the Spirit of God recreates you from above as He descends upon you like a dove. He is a Gentleman.

> Behold, I stand at the door, and knock: if any man hear my voice, and open the door, I will come in to him and will sup with him, and he with me.
>
> Revelation 3:20

Will you ask Jesus into your heart today? If you have already made a commitment, is it time for a renewal? Do you need or would you like times of refreshing?

A born again child of God is created in the image of Love Himself.

> And hope maketh not ashamed; because the love of God is shed abroad in our hearts by the Holy Ghost which is given unto us.
>
> Romans 5:5

So why do Christians struggle? Obviously, there are many reasons but let's look into this a little bit to obtain some clarification.

In 1 Peter 1:23 we read,

> Being born again, not of corruptible seed but
> of incorruptible, by the word of God which
> liveth and abideth forever.

This is our true essence as we are spirit beings that have received an indestructible nature once we have accepted Jesus into our hearts.

However, there is still a process of the development of our souls which is separate from our spirits which we will see shortly in 1 Thessalonians 5:23. Our souls are essentially comprised of our mental faculties.

One of our main objectives is to allow the Holy Spirit to bridge the gap between our spirits and souls so that they are in complete unity.

"Receiving the end of your faith, even the salvation of your souls." (1 Peter 1:9)

How are we to be successful with this endeavor? By continually searching for the truth found in the holy Word of God.

> This Book of the Law shall not depart out of
> thy mouth; but thou shalt meditate therein
> day and night, that thou mayest observe to
> do according to all that is written therein: for
> then thou shalt make thy way prosperous, and
> then thou shalt have good success.
>
> Joshua 1:8

This helps our spirits, souls, minds and bodies to prosper which leads to a beautiful transformation because of a continual renewal from within.

"The righteous shall flourish like the palm tree..." (Psalm 92:12)

Time is critical for the Body of Christ to come out of the cocoon and be transformed by taking on the wings of love and flying to our destinies. This can be done at the speed of light if we will all submit and be obedient to His will.

> But as he which hath called you is holy, so be ye holy in all manner of conversation; Because it is written, Be ye holy; for I am holy.
>
> 1 Peter 1:15–16

If you truly want to have eternal life, you must believe in Jesus and receive what He has already provided for you. Will you accept this free gift of love? Your life literally depends on it.

> For God so loved the world that he gave his only begotten Son, that whosoever believeth in him should not perish, but have everlasting life.
>
> John 3:16

It does not matter what you have done in the past as you cannot escape the depths of His unconditional love. Ask Him into your heart today and allow Him to wash your sins away. You will feel new and see a beautiful view from within you.

> For God did not send his Son into the world to condemn the world, but that the world through him might be saved.
>
> John 3:17

Will you come into His light? Will you allow Him to set you free and make you complete? Would you like those around you to see His truth and light? Then submit to His ways all of your days and you will truly be amazed of all of His accomplishments that will soon take place.

We belong to and are one with Love.

It certainly is time to allow Him to fulfill His will and to "be still, and know that I am God..." (Psalm 46:10)

We can then rest and allow Him to become more within us so we can truly become less. "He must increase, but I must decrease." (John 3:30)

When this occurs, we can find a peace that can only come from above which is heavenly.

Finally, Love is a force. Let's stand up for what is right and watch the enemy take flight. Will you walk with His Spirit Who is without limit? Let's take off all of the limitations today.

> And the very God of peace sanctify you wholly; and I pray your whole spirit and soul and body be preserved blameless unto the coming of our LORD Jesus Christ. Faithful is he that calleth you, who also will do it.
>
> 1 Thessalonians 5:23–24

Jesus says,

> And, behold, I come quickly; and my reward is with me, to give to every man according as his work shall be.
>
> Revelation 22:12

Chapter 4

It is interesting to note that Jesus conversed with a Samaritan woman who came to draw water from a well. She was astonished that a Jew would even talk to a Samaritan. (See John 4:9.)

We tend to look at people from the outward appearance but Jesus always looks at the heart from within.

Jesus asked this woman a simple question. Of course, she looked at the natural due to the fact she truly did not know Who Love was and is. (See John 4:7.)

His response was so beautiful. Love offered her "living water" that would quench all of the desert places and provide her with the ultimate oasis. (See John 4:10–14.)

This same offer is for us today. Will you ask Him to fill you with His "living water" to overflowing so that there is no longer a dry area in your life? This is certainly a powerful possibility.

It is also worth noting that this woman was not living in a godly way. Did Love act as we tend to do by judging others based upon natural origins of what we see and hear? No, Jesus saw her hurting heart and that she was open to the living Spirit of love and truth. As a matter of fact, Jesus was very clear when He said,

> But the hour cometh, and now is, when the true worshippers shall worship the Father in spirit and in truth: for the Father seeketh such to worship him. God is a spirit: and they that worship him must worship him in spirit and in truth.
>
> John 4:23–24

This woman then said that she was looking for the Messiah. (See John 4:25.) "Jesus saith unto her, I that speak unto thee am he." (John 4:26)

> This same woman went back to town and said to the people, "Come, see a man, which told me all things that I ever did: is not this the Christ?
>
> John 4:29

> And many of the Samaritans of that city believed on him for the saying of the woman, which testified, He told me all that I ever did. So when the Samaritans were come unto him, they besought him that he would tarry with

> them: and he abode there two days. And many
> more believed because of his own word; And
> said unto the woman, Now we believe, not
> because of thy saying: for we have heard him
> ourselves, and know that this is indeed the
> Christ, the Saviour of the world.
>
> John 4:39–42

Jesus shared an additional truth with His disciples when He said, "My meat is to do the will of him that sent me and to finish his work." (John 4:34)

It is certainly time for us to open our eyes and see that the nations are perfectly ripe for the picking. (See John 4:35.)

Every day, our loving Father provides us with outstanding opportunities to express His heart with those around us. Many times, we are too blind to see due to our lack of sensitivity to His compassionate Spirit.

Let's repent for our indifference and to truly make a difference for His kingdom of light.

Allow Love's miracles to flow through you as Jesus will draw people to you to portray His cascading drops of sweet morning dew.

> So Jesus came again into Cana of Galilee,
> where he made the water wine. And there
> was a certain nobleman, whose son was sick

at Capernaum. When he heard that Jesus was come out of Judaea into Galilee, he went unto him, and besought him that he would come down, and heal his son: for he was at the point of death. Then said Jesus unto him, Except ye see signs and wonders, ye will not believe. The nobleman saith unto him, Sir, come down ere my child die. Jesus saith unto him, Go thy way; thy son liveth. And the man believed the word that Jesus had spoken unto him, and he went his way. And as he was now going down, his servants met him, and told him, saying, Thy son liveth. Then enquired he of them the hour when he began to amend. And they said unto him, Yesterday at the seventh hour the fever left him. So the father knew that it was at the same hour, in which Jesus said unto him, Thy son liveth: and himself believed, and his whole house. This is again the second miracle that Jesus did, when he was come out of Judae into Galilee.

John 4:46–54

Chapter 5

> And a certain man was there, which had an
> infirmity thirty and eight years. When Jesus
> saw him lie, and knew that he had been now a
> long time in that case, he saith unto him, Wilt
> thou be made whole?
>
> John 5:5–6

Do we ask those around us who are crippled physically, emotionally, socially or financially if they want to become complete? Even more to the heart of the matter, Love is asking all of us if we want to be full of all that is good.

In order for us to love others, we must believe, receive and perceive His love personally before we can show this to those around us.

Let's get back to the individual mentioned at the beginning of this chapter.

> Jesus saith unto him, Rise, take up thy bed,
> and walk. And immediately the man was made
> whole, and took up his bed, and walked...
>
> John 5:8–9

Obviously, Jesus perceived this person had the faith to be healed. Do we look for opportunities to be bold enough to pray for the sick who are looking for a healing?

Now Jesus healed on the Sabbath, so the religious folks persecuted Him and were looking for ways to kill Him. (See John 5:16.)

Religion tends to destroy the essence of a very intimate relationship with our Father. Why? It cannot comprehend unconditional love as we will discuss shortly in the upcoming verses.

A religious spirit is deceptive as it portrays godliness but it certainly lacks the power to bring forth life.

We can do great things for God by speaking words of liberty, life and love into all situations.

We bring honor to our Father by believing what He says and by following His examples of love and authority.

Do you want to be free from condemnation? Then please listen carefully to the following words of edification from Jesus:

> Verily, verily, I say unto you, He that heareth my word, and believeth on him that sent me, hath everlasting life, and shall not come into condemnation; but is passed from death unto life.
>
> John 5:24

> For he saith, I have heard thee in a time accepted, and in the day of salvation have I succoured thee: behold, now is the accepted time; behold, now is the day of salvation.
>
> II Corinthians 6:2

If we truly want to live life to the fullest, it is crucial that we believe that this is the right time to inherit His abundant ways of living.

Will we make the right choice and listen intuitively to His voice?

You can live a holy life based upon Philippians 4:13 which states "I can do all things through Christ which strengtheneth me."

"...For when I am weak, then am I strong." (II Corinthians 12:10)

Let's all stop believing the enemy's lies as Colossians 2:15 states

> And having spoiled principalities and powers, he made a shew of them openly, triumphing over them in it.

The enemy and all of his lost companions have already been defeated. Let's focus on the truth found in God's words of victorious love.

Look to the One Who was hung on a tree and truly experience all He has done to set you free.

Jesus always looks to please our Father. If we will take the same attitude and come up to a higher altitude, we will partake of a freedom like no other.

All of us are called to "trust in the LORD, and do good…" (Psalm 37:3)

What good works are we doing to bring Him glory?

Also, are His words living abundantly within us?

> Let the word of Christ dwell in you richly in all wisdom; teaching and admonishing one another in psalms and hymns and spiritual songs, singing with grace in your hearts to the LORD. And whatsoever ye do in word or deed, do all in the name of the LORD Jesus, giving thanks to God and the Father by him.
>
> Colossians 3:16–17

Who is Jesus to you?

> But of him are ye in Christ Jesus, who of God
> is made unto us wisdom, and righteousness,
> and sanctification, and redemption.
>
> 1 Corinthians 1:30

Love truly is all encompassing.

Come to Jesus today in a special way and receive His illuminating essence by bathing in His purest presence. This will truly make you clean from all of the pollutants of the world. Yes, the truth is you cannot remain stagnant. For the world will take you downstream and further away from Love but if you swim upstream you will attain to a higher level above.

Do not look for the praises of people. This will only lead to disappointment as society is always looking for a new flavor to savor. They are looking for ways to satisfy the emptiness that can only be satisfied with His passion of purity.

I pray that the Spirit of God ignites a holy fire within us so that we can shine ever so brightly, this day and always.

Chapter 6

Is Jesus speaking to you today? Is Love asking you questions about your life as He asked individuals when He walked on this earth?

You might ask, "How can this be? For Jesus is not physically walking on this earth."

If you are a born again child of God, His Spirit is living within you, desiring to fellowship with you. If you will be quiet from within, you can listen to Him speaking to your heart as Love communicates Spirit to spirit.

If you have never made a firm decision to ask Jesus into your heart, now is the best time to open up and accept His gracious invitation. Please don't go by your mind, looking at life from an intellectual standpoint.

I believe Jesus is waiting for you to open up to the realm of the miraculous. Do you believe?

If so, take a moment and ask Him into your heart. Bathe in His loving presence.

If you have already made a commitment, would you like to come up to a higher level? Would you like to excel in all you do for His glory? You will need to submit and lift up your hearts to attain a freedom that is indescribable.

How do we expect to do miracles such as the feeding of the thousands? (See John 6:5–12.) We limit Love Himself with our finite minds saying, "Well, that was Jesus. Surely we can't expect to do the same things Jesus did." Actually, we can but I am getting ahead of myself. We will discuss this further in Chapter 14. For now, feel free to look at John 14:12 for a confirmation of this point of view.

Let's look a little more closely at the feeding of the thousands. Jesus made a fascinating statement after they all had enough to eat. Love said, "Gather up the fragments that remain, that nothing be lost." (John 6:12)

Do you know that Jesus does not waste a single moment of your life? He will heal all of the wounds and scars and show you that He is "...the bright and morning star." (Revelation 22:16)

Do you honestly think Love will discard your hurts as if they are irrelevant? No, He is waiting to make you totally whole. (See Luke 4:18.)

What do you do when the storms of life come? (See John 6:18.)

Jesus is saying to us too, "It is I; be not afraid." (John 6:20)

How can I say this?

"Jesus Christ the same yesterday, and to day, and for ever." (Hebrews 13:8)

Plus, "…God is no respecter of persons." (Acts 10:34)

All Love asks is "…that ye believe on him whom he hath sent." (John 6:29) It truly is up to you.

Will you put away all doubts?

If you will do this, you will start to see Jesus is with you, helping you to reach the divine destination He beautifully has planned for you.

Is it worth the price to settle for life's temporary pleasures?

We will all stand before Him for what we have done or not done. Thank goodness, it is not too late if we have missed it. It is a simple matter of repentance and acceptance of Love's compassion, forgiveness and mercy.

Will you ask Him for a revelation of this today?

> And Jesus said unto them, I am the bread of life: he that cometh to me shall never hunger; and he that believeth on me shall never thirst.
>
> John 6:35

Are there any areas in your life that are not completely satisfied? Yes, of course.

If we will fellowship with our Father by studying His Word, praising Him, listening to and obeying His voice, we will start to experience this fulfillment of Love. I assure you, nothing on this earth can even come close. It is like day and night if you can catch sight of His light.

Let's do His will and not our own. (See John 6:38.)

This leads us to another area when it comes to faith. How do I know God's will as compared to my own? This can only be accomplished by truly having an intimate relationship with the God of all creation. He will lead, guide and direct you every step of the way.

"And let the peace of God rule in your hearts..." (Colossians 3:15)

It's time for all of us to set aside our own preconceived ideas. Why? Jesus said,

> It is the spirit that quickeneth; the flesh profiteth nothing: the words that I speak unto you, they are spirit, and they are life.
>
> John 6:63

Will you do this today?

Chapter 7

Wisdom knows where danger lurks and stays away, not allowing an open door to the enemy of deceit.

Even Jesus purposely stayed away from a particular town when it was known that a group of people were waiting to take Love's life. (See John 7:1.)

Jesus lived a perfect life while He walked on this earth, yet even his own brothers did not have faith in Him. (See John 7:5.) How much more can this happen to us who do not live perfectly?

When you speak the truth, be prepared for opposition from the world. (See John 7:7.)

What is most important is that we fulfill His will as Love "…hath committed unto us the word of reconciliation." (11 Corinthians 5:19)

> He that speaketh of himself seeketh his own
> glory: but he that seeketh his glory that sent

him, the same is true, and no unrighteousness
is in him.

John 7:18

It is not a matter of trying to fulfill every aspect of the Law but to want to please our Father in all that we think or do. Will you allow Love to accomplish all He wants to do for you?

The time is short. Jesus is coming soon. Are you ready to see Him face to face? In all honesty, we face Love everyday as "…he that is joined unto the LORD is one spirit." (1 Corinthians 6:17)

Jesus said,

…If any man thirst, let him come unto me,
and drink. He that believeth on me, as the
scripture hath said, out of his belly shall flow
rivers of living water.

John 7:37–38

As noted above, if you are thirsty, come and drink of His purifying ways which are totally satisfying.

You can have such an impact within and without your immediate circles. Your spheres of influence can increase if you are interested.

Do you want to be all He has created you to be?

"Stand fast therefore in the liberty wherewith Christ hath made us free…" (Galatians 5:1)

Chapter 8

And early in the morning he came again into
the temple, and all the people came unto him;
and he sat down and taught them.

John 8:1

A few thoughts come to mind when I reflect upon the
above passage of scripture:

Are we willing to wake up early to spend time with
Love? Plus, do we put Jesus first?

It is crucial to fellowship with our Father before we
partake of life's daily activities. How do we expect to
obtain wisdom to make the right choices if we have not
taken time to listen to the Spirit of God?

We can enjoy such an awesome time with Him if we
are willing to experience sweet communion with His
Majesty.

Love will brighten your day and lighten your way if
you will commit to Him this day.

It is critical to note John 8:3–11. Let's take a look at Light's point of view of this amazing story that is all to His glory.

Religious leaders brought a woman to Jesus, who had committed a particular sin. (See John 8:3.)

According to the Law, she should have been stoned. (See John 8:5.) They were also trying to trap Jesus with His own words. (See John 8:6.) The religious leaders were relentless so Jesus responded, "… He that is without sin among you, let him first cast a stone at her." (John 8:7)

What gives us the right to look at each other's sins through the eyes of the Law?

We truly need to look at our own lives and deal with our own sins and to allow the Spirit of Love to convict other people of their own sins.

When we begin to live holy lives, others will see His light within us. This will certainly open doors to share His magnificent love which will lead other individuals to repentance. (See Romans 2:4.)

Getting back to the woman caught in a specific sin. When Jesus asked the leaders of the time the question noted in John 8:7 above, they all left except for the woman that was cast before Jesus.

What Love said after the accusations was remarkable:

"Neither do I condemn thee: go, and sin no more." (John 8:11)

This is what will bring true transformation to others. Conviction will always draw people closer to God while condemnation will drive them away. This can be easily proven. How? Just think for a moment. Since when has the devil's tactics ever been blessed by Love? It is the enemy who brings false accusations. (See Revelation 12:10.)

Jesus said,

> ...I am the light of the world: he that followeth me shall not walk in darkness, but shall have the light of life.
>
> John 8:12

It is time for us to allow Love to shed light upon the dark areas of our lives. He will not embarrass you but He will empower you to walk the perfect paths that only He can establish.

Do we know of Jesus or do we truly know Him by having a living and breathing relationship with the very essence of life Himself?

Let's leave our life of sin and embrace Him. Our Father will come running with open arms of love and carry you away to a place far above. (See Luke 15:11–32.)

Our Father is waiting for us. What are we waiting for? This is the opportunity to obtain fresh revelation from heaven about who you can become in Christ. More of Him, less of us. It is a matter of trust.

Jesus said,

> …If ye continue in my word, then are ye my disciples indeed; And ye shall know the truth, and the truth shall make you free. If the Son therefore shall make you free, ye shall be free indeed.
>
> John 8:31–32, 36

So what is freedom? From what I perceive from above, it is the ability to know and recognize that we can truly walk on this earth without having to be in bondage to what is contrary to Love.

Sin is selfish. Godly love is liberating.

We should look at what we can do for our Father's creation as compared to what we can receive from them. "…It is more blessed to give than to receive." (Acts 20:35)

It is up to us to make the right choices on a continual basis. If we choose to do what is right, we will receive the abundance of blessings our Father has in store for us. (See Deuteronomy 28:1–14.)

If we choose to love, what force can stand up to this and win?

Too many people are searching to satisfy their cravings, longings and desires with things that are only temporary.

The only way to be complete is to receive His love, express this gift back to Him and to love others which includes walking in forgiveness.

Love and forgiveness cannot be separated as they go hand in hand.

The story found in Luke 7:36–50 provides a beautiful portrayal of love, forgiveness, faith and peace.

Come to Love with all of your flaws and allow Him to show you the person you were created to be.

Ask for forgiveness and choose to forgive so that you can truly live.

If Jesus has forgiven us, shouldn't we do the same towards those who have hurt us? Of course.

It is time to for us to accept the reality of His forgiving ways and to allow Him to purify us from all of the toxins that have polluted our own ideas.

"For who hath known the mind of the LORD, that he may instruct him? But we have the mind of Christ." (1 Corinthians 2:16)

Isn't it time we start thinking like Jesus?

Let's be a precise reflection of Him by mirroring His love and light so that the world can catch sight of this wonderful delight.

Rejoice in the LORD alway: and again I say, Rejoice. Be careful for nothing; but in every thing by prayer and supplication with thanksgiving let your requests be made known unto God. And the peace of God, which passeth all understanding, shall keep your hearts and minds through Christ Jesus. I can do all things through Christ which strengtheneth me.

Philippians 4:4, 6–7, 13

If you will follow His concepts, you will live in a way you never thought possible.

Love is forever present to help you in all you do for Him.

If the religious folks pick up their spiritual rocks, ask Jesus to shield you so that you can fulfill your purpose. (See John 8:59.)

Chapter 9

When you look at the miracle of the man that was born blind in John 9:1–7, you see that Jesus healed him in a way that was not typical. After performing an act that would not be considered to be orthodox, Love gave the man specific instructions. It was after the man obeyed the words of Jesus that he received his sight.

It is also imperative that we follow the words of Jesus completely.

Do we want all He has for us or just a sampling of His goodness?

In John 9:13–34, we see that the religious leaders repeatedly questioned the man who received Love's miracle. The man was not afraid to speak the truth, even when he was insulted. They eventually threw the man out of their presence.

Have you been thrown away by a family member, a relative or by others?

"Jesus heard that they had cast him out; and when

he had found him, he said unto him, Dost thou believe on the Son of God?" (John 9:35)

Do you believe that Jesus is looking for you?

Some of you are not to blame for the transgressions and trespasses that were forced upon you. Will you bring Him all of the pain and shame?

Jesus made another impeccable statement when He said, "…For judgment I am come into this world, that they which see not might see…" (John 9:39)

Yes, now is the best time to open your eyes to see the special gifts Love has to offer to you.

Chapter 10

Love is calling you by name. Jesus is guiding you towards the most fertile fields so that you can find rest in Him. (See John 10:3, 9; Psalm 23:2.)

Let's take a closer look at Psalm 23 for just a few moments:

> The LORD is my shepherd; I shall not want. He maketh me to lie down in green pastures: he leadeth me beside the still waters. He restoreth my soul: he leadeth me in the paths of righteousness for his name's sake. Yea, thou I walk through the valley of the shadow of death, I will fear no evil: for thou art with me; thy rod and thy staff they comfort me. Thou preparest a table before me in the presence of mine enemies: thou anointest my head with oil; my cup runneth over. Surely goodness and mercy

shall follow me all the days of my life: and I
will dwell in the house of the LORD for ever.

When we study the above passage, we can see that
Love is willing to provide us with times of relaxation
and refreshment.

We can also see that we are never alone as
Love is always with us to shed light upon all of our
circumstances.

In John 10:10 Jesus clearly states,

The thief cometh not, but for to steal, and to
kill, and to destroy: I am come that they might
have life, and that they might have it more
abundantly.

If the Body of Christ will meditate on the above
scripture, it would set us free from so many false tradi-
tions set up by individuals. This concept is so simple
that we tend to complicate this truth with our own rea-
soning and false beliefs.

"I am the God…of the living." (Matthew 22:32)

Love is full of life, not death. With this in mind, let's
stop all of the divisions of why we think God allowed
this or that. We will all stand before Jesus one day and
then we will fully know the truth with respect to our
walks on this earth.

"I am the good shepherd: the good shepherd giveth his life for the sheep." (John 10:11)

Jesus did this willingly for you and me as Love originally created us to be a family of one.

> Behold, what manner of love the Father hath bestowed upon us, that we should be called the sons of God…
>
> 1 John 3:1

Are we willing to fully give our lives to the One Who is only interested in helping us to become the dynamic individuals He created us to be?

I truly believe our Father has placed this book before you so you can become more acquainted with Love.

Do you ever ask Him questions about His very essence? Do you ask Him how you can get to know Him better? The more you understand Who He is, the better you will understand yourself as you have been made in Love's very "…own image…" (Genesis 1:27)

Please do not always come to God asking Him for stuff. Our Father is interested in giving us His best but He wants us to have the right objectives.

"But seek ye first the kingdom of God, and his righteousness; and all these things shall be added unto you." (Matthew 6:33)

Praise Him with all of your heart. Glorify Him for

all He has done, is continually doing and will do in the future.

Look around and see the miracles of life. This could only have been done by the Creator of all creation.

If you have made a quality decision to accept Jesus into your heart, no one can take you out of Love's firm grasp. (See John 10:27–29.)

Jesus said, "I and my Father are one." (John 10:30)

You know what? You are one with Love too. (See John 17:21.)

Some people will think you are nuts. If the religious leaders picked up stones to attempt to stone Jesus, Who is perfect, what do you think they will do to us? Yes, some will pick up their spiritual stones and try to throw them at us but Jesus will provide a protective path. (See John 6:31–39.)

Also, be encouraged, for many will come to Him through our testimony to His loving ways. (See John 10:42.)

No, we are not God, but we should become more like Him.

Let's share the greatest miracle of all, the gift of eternal life.

> Therefore if any man be in Christ, he is a new
> creature: old things are passed away; behold,
> all things are become new. And all things are

of God, who hath reconciled us to himself by Jesus Christ, and hath given unto us the ministry of reconciliation; To wit, that God was in Christ, reconciling the world unto himself, not imputing their trespasses unto them; and hath committed unto us the word of reconciliation. Now then we are ambassadors for Christ, as though God did beseech you by us: we pray you in Christ's stead, be ye reconciled to God. For he hath made him to be sin for us, who knew no sin; that we might be made the righteousness of God in him.

II Corinthians 5:17–21

If we confess our sins, he is faithful and just to forgive us our sins, and to cleanse us from all unrighteousness.

I John 1:9

Chapter 11

Love desires to have a very intimate relationship with you.

"For our God is a consuming fire." (Hebrews 12:29)

He will set you free from all types of sickness and the areas of death that keep you buried underneath your true potential.

Lazarus was a perfect example of this truth. (See John 11:1–45.)

Sickness does not have to end in death. Sometimes tragedies do take place. Yet, if these individuals were Christians, they have received the ultimate healing. They are totally free and are glorifying our God in heaven. It is us who are left behind that sometimes suffer.

In the story of Lazarus, we see the love of Jesus exemplified as well as faith. Galatians 5:6 states, "…Faith…worketh by love."

We also see that people's perspectives are obviously

different. What is most important is that we keep our focus on Jesus.

John 11:17 states, "Then when Jesus came, he found that he had lain in the grave four days already."

What tombs are you still lying in?

In John 11:25–26, Jesus voiced these words which still hold true today:

> I am the resurrection, and the life: he that believeth in me, though he were dead, yet shall he live. And whosoever liveth and believeth in me shall never die. Believest thou this?

Do you believe Love can raise to life your hopes and dreams?

> Now unto him that is able to do exceeding abundantly above all that we ask or think, according to the power that worketh in us.
> Ephesians 3:20

When Mary heard that Love was asking for her, "…she arose quickly, and came unto him." (John 11:29)

Jesus is asking for you too. Will you get up immediately and open up your heart to Him?

> Jesus said, Take ye away the stone. Martha, the sister of him that was dead, saith unto him, LORD, by this time he stinketh: for he hath been dead four days.
>
> John 11:39

The longer we wait in our tombs that contradict His love, the less likely we will emit a sweet fragrance that will attract others to him.

In John 11:40, we read that Love did not focus on the negativity expressed by Martha as he asked, "…Said I not unto thee, that, if thou wouldest believe, thou shouldest see the glory of God?"

> Then they took away the stone from the place where the dead was laid. And Jesus lifted up his eyes, and said, Father, I thank thee that thou hast heard me. And I knew that thou hearest me always: but because of the people which stand by I said it, that they may believe that thou hast sent me. And when he thus had spoken, he cried with a loud voice, Lazarus, come forth. And he that was dead came forth, bound hand and foot with graveclothes: and his face was bound about with a napkin. Jesus saith unto them, Loose him, and let him go. Then many of the Jews which

came to Mary, and had seen the things which
Jesus did, believed on him.

John 11:41–45

It is time for us to take off the clothes that keep us
bound and to pursue our Father's passions that pertain
to purity. Will we choose to believe?

Chapter 12

Then took Mary a pound of ointment of spike-
nard, very costly, and anointed the feet of
Jesus, and wiped his feet with her hair: and the
house was filled with the odour of the ointment. Then saith one of his disciples, Judas
Iscariot, Simon's son, which should betray
him, Why was not this ointment sold for
three hundred pence, and given to the poor?
This he said, not that he cared for the poor;
but because he was a thief, and had the bag,
and bare what was put therein. Then said Jesus,
Let her alone: against the day of my burying
hath she kept this. For the poor always ye have
with you; but me ye have not always.

John 12:3–8

Love has called you to do things that have been ordained
from the beginning of time.

Don't allow the enemy to try and steal your God-given abilities, talents and instructions.

Our Father will give you the necessary strength and shield you from the liar's tactics.

You can become a sweet fragrance for our Creator.

Bask in His presence and partake of His essence.

This will also provide you with the opportunity of discernment to escape the enemy's traps.

Why do we continually resist coming to Love? We tend to be afraid for many reasons. One primary factor is sin. We act like our Father is ready to punish us when we come to Him to confess our sins.

> But God commendeth his love toward us, in that, while we were yet sinners, Christ died for us. Much more then, being now justified by his blood, we shall be saved from wrath through him. For if, when we were enemies, we were reconciled to God by the death of his Son, much more, being reconciled, we shall be saved by his life.
>
> Romans 5:8–10

Listen, Jesus left His glory to tell His story.

> Who being the brightness of his glory, and the express image of his person, and upholding all

things by the word of his power, when he had by himself purged our sins, sat down at the right hand of the Majesty on high.

Hebrews 1:3

Let's continue to look at the Book of John.

And Jesus answered them, saying, The hour is come, that the Son of man should be glorified. Verily, verily, I say unto you, Except a corn of wheat fall into the ground and die, it abideth alone: but if it die, it bringeth forth much fruit. He that loveth his life shall lose it; and he that hateth his life in this world shall keep it unto life eternal. If any man serve me, let him follow me; and where I am, there shall also my servant be: if any man serve me, him will my Father honour.

John 12:23–26

If any of us expects to receive His glory, we must allow ourselves to die in areas that are not producing exceptional and bountiful fruit.

Let's allow Him to save us in every way today.

Now is my soul troubled; and what shall I say? Father, save me from this hour: but for this cause came I unto this hour.

John 12:27

Jesus knew beforehand all that would take place in the future before He came to this earth.

His heart was troubled as He knew it was almost time to be led to a horrible death. Yet, Love knew it was for this purpose He came to this earth. Why? So we would not have to face eternal separation from Love Himself.

If people could only see this truth, they would come flocking into His fold and not continue to be sold into slavery.

There is no freedom in walking along the dark paths.

Our Father cannot and will not bless what has been cursed.

"…The prince of this world…" has already been sentenced to death. (John 12:31)

Do not allow the enemy to try and pass part of this sentence on to you.

Hell was created for Satan and the fallen angels. (See Revelation 20:10.)

It was never ever meant for people to inhabit this desolate location.

Unfortunately, people still choose to believe the lies which lead to their ultimate demise.

Please, do not allow this to happen to you or to those you love.

Jesus is still guiding each and every person to Himself as He is preparing their hearts to receive His love. (See John 12:32.)

Be sensitive to the Holy Spirit as He will provide opportunities for you to share Love's greatest gift on a daily basis.

Of course, there will always be skeptics as is evidenced in John 12:34.

It is important for us to continue to trust in His might and to be a strong reflection of His light.

This leads us to an important question. Are we looking for the acceptance and admiration of people or from the One Who deserves all of our adoration? (See John 12:43.)

Our Father will honor you if you look to please Him. (See 1 Peter 5:6.)

If we look to His living light, we can receive true sight. This will allow us to focus on what truly matters in life.

What would this be? To help all of our Father's creation. To love, to serve, to protect and to provide. Oh, what a glorious ride.

If you want the time of your life, put away the strife and look to be a blessing to others.

Focus on what you can do as compared to what you think you can't do.

Generally, those who have accomplished much have faced great challenges. Yet, they absolutely refused to give up. We are reaping their benefits. It is time for us to sow endurance too so we can see the abundant harvest that Love has for us.

"…If God be for us, who can be against us?" (Romans 8:31)

Listen to His words, hear what He has to say, speak with love and authority to those who walk your way.

Love and obedience go hand in hand so it is time for us to do what He commands.

> And I know that his commandment is life everlasting: whatsoever I speak therefore, even as the Father said unto me, so I speak.
>
> John 12:50

Chapter 13

"For I have given you an example, that ye should do as I have done to you." (John 13:15)

"If ye know these things, happy are ye if ye do them." (John 13:17)

Let's freely flow in what has been bestowed upon us from above.

We ask why He has allowed certain events to take place on this earth. When in reality, He can ask the same of us.

> And Jesus came and spake unto them, saying, All power is given unto me in heaven and earth. Go ye therefore, and teach all nations, baptizing them in the name of the Father, and of the Son, and of the Holy Ghost: Teaching them to observe all things whatsoever I have commanded you: and lo, I am with you alway, even unto the end of the world. Amen.
>
> Matthew 28:18–20

We have a major responsibility to express His truths to a world that is searching for answers.

Do we show this message?

First, we truly have to believe before we can mirror this truth to a world of falsehood.

Jesus knew beforehand we would betray Him. Yes, betray Him. Every time we sin, we betray His goodness and compassion. Yet, He always has a passion for us to come back into the fold and not to scold.

> The LORD is gracious, and full of compassion; slow to anger, and of great mercy. The LORD is good to all: and his tender mercies are over all his works.
>
> Psalm 145:8–9

Are we doing the same or are we quick to show anger and judgment?

"…Freely ye have received, freely give." (Matthew 10:8)

There is so much more for us to do.

It is so important for us to have the right attitude and to come up to a much higher terrain.

If necessary, let's ask for forgiveness at this defining moment of our walks with Love.

> Come now, and let us reason together, saith
> the LORD: though your sins be as scarlet, they
> shall be as white as snow; though they be red
> like crimson, they shall be as wool.
>
> Isaiah 1:18

"Who forgiveth all thine iniquities; who healeth all thy diseases." (Psalm 103:2)

"As far as the east is from the west, so far hath he removed our transgressions from us." (Psalm 103:12)

When Love forgives, He chooses to forget.

Can we accept this for ourselves and then show the same beauty towards others?

> A new commandment I give unto you, That
> ye love one another; as I have loved you, that
> ye also love one another. By this shall all men
> know that ye are my disciples, if ye have love
> one to another.
>
> John 13:34–35

We have two choices when we abandon Love. Will we act like Judas or Peter? (See Matthew 27:3–5; 69–75.)

You can see the transformation of Peter's life if you will study the Book of Acts.

For those of us who love God, I know we truly want to do what is right.

If we fall, let's be quick to repent. If we have been hurt, let's be quick to forgive.

Oftentimes, people that have been hurt will either hurt others or themselves.

Love can heal all if we will allow Him to.

As we freely receive His Love, we can then express this same love towards our heavenly Father. It is only then that we can fully open up our arms and love those around us. This is the form of the cross. It starts vertically and extends horizontally.

Chapter 14

Jesus also said,

> Let not your hearts be troubled: ye believe in
> God, believe also in me. In my Father's house
> are many mansions: if it were not so, I would
> have told you. I go to prepare a place for you.
> And if I go and prepare a place for you, I will
> come again, and receive you unto myself; that
> where I am, there ye may be also. And wither I
> go ye know, and the way ye know.
>
> John 14:1–4

"I am the way, the truth, and the life: no man cometh
unto the Father, but by me." (John 14:6)

"Every word of God is pure: he is a shield unto them
that put their trust in him." (Proverbs 30:5)

It's time for us to trust our Father and to believe we
will be with Him for eternity.

Let's follow His ways which are the best opportunities that could ever be presented to us.

He is living within us if we have opened up our hearts to Him.

> Verily, verily, I say unto you, He that believeth on me, the works that I do shall he do also; and greater works than these shall he do; because I go unto my Father.
>
> John 14:12

Let's take a look at Ephesians 1:15–18 for a moment as I believe the two references go hand in hand:

> Wherefore I also, after I heard of your faith in the LORD Jesus, and love unto all the saints, Cease not to give thanks for you, making mention of you in my prayers; That the God of our LORD Jesus Christ, the Father of glory, may give unto you the spirit of wisdom and revelation in the knowledge of him: The eyes of your understanding being enlightened; that ye may know what is the hope of his calling, and what the riches of the glory of his inheritance in the saints.

This truly is the highest calling and will open up doors for us to do what Love did as He walked on this earth. Plus, we can do even more if we will believe and grow in our walks with Him.

> If ye love me, keep my commandments.
>
> John 14:15

> And whatsoever ye shall ask in my name, that will I do, that the Father may be glorified in the Son. If ye shall ask anything in my name, I will do it.
>
> John 14:13–14

What could bring more glory to our Father than to ask Him to help us to love Him openly and to be obedient to all He instructs of us?

This is what life is all about.

> Jesus said unto him, Thou shalt love the LORD thy God with all thy heart, and with all thy soul, and with all thy mind. This is the first and great commandment. And the second is like unto it, Thou shalt love thy neighbour as thyself. On these two commandments hang all the law and the prophets.
>
> Matthew 22:37–40

How is this possible? Let's look at John 14:17, 26 to find out:

> Even the Spirit of truth; whom the world cannot receive, because it seeth him not, neither knoweth him: but ye know him; for he dwelleth with you, and shall be in you. But the Comforter, which is the Holy Ghost, whom the Father will send in my name, he shall teach you all things, and bring all things to your remembrance, whatsoever I have said unto you.

The very next words that come out of the mouth of Jesus are as follows:

> Peace I leave with you, my peace I give unto you: not as the world giveth, give I unto you. Let not your hearts be troubled, neither let it be afraid.
>
> John 14:27

The Holy Spirit will always bring peace so rejoice. He is our Friend Who has been sent to help us to better understand Love and all of His ways.

Let's explore this truth even further.

Continuing with the words of Jesus:

> He that hath my commandments, and keepeth them, he it is that loveth me: and he that loveth me shall be loved of my Father, and I will love him, and will manifest myself to him.
>
> John 14:21

> ...If a man love me, he will keep my words: and my Father will love him, and we will come unto him, and make our abode with him.
>
> John 14:23

Do you truly feel at home with Jesus? Do you feel complete?

If not, will you take this opportunity to allow Him to love you unconditionally?

I believe He wants to bring us all up to a much higher level of excellence.

With this in mind, we can also obtain a peace that is truly satisfying.

Jesus also said "...The prince of this world...hath nothing in me." (John 14:30)

It is time for us to stop allowing the enemy to have any control over us according to the words of Jesus also found in John 17:21:

> That they all may be one; as thou, Father, art in me, and I in thee, that they also may

be one in us: that the world may believe that
thou has sent me.

We are one with Love, Who is also one with us.
Let's live by the truth contained in the above.

Chapter 15

Jesus said,

> I am the true vine, and my Father is the hus-
> bandman. Every branch in me that beareth
> not fruit he taketh away: and every branch
> that beareth fruit, he purgeth it, that it may
> bring forth more fruit.
>
> John 15:1–2

First of all, it is of the utmost importance that we truly believe that Jesus is our very essence of life.

Second, let's be thankful that Love is available to purge us from all of the dead works that have hindered us from walking holy paths.

The only requirement is that we ask.

Love waits very patiently for us to open up every area that we have not fully committed to him.

Are we willing to show the same amount of patience?

Love has given us invaluable gifts.

It is up to us to develop these talents and to attain our fullest potential. Let's strive to fully come alive.

Jesus also said, "Now ye are clean through the word which I have spoken unto you." (John 15:3)

Let's allow Love to cleanse us with His purifying words of life.

In John 15:4–6 we find words that will bring true humility if we will totally comprehend Love's position as compared to ours. Let's read these powerful truths:

> Abide in me, and I in you. As the branch cannot bear fruit of itself, except it abide in the vine; no more can ye, except ye abide in me. I am the vine, ye are the branches: He that abideth in me, and I in him, the same bringeth forth much fruit: for without me you can do nothing. If a man abide not in me, he is cast forth as a branch, and is withered; and men gather them, and cast them into the fire, and they are burned.

All gifts, talents, abilities and special qualities have been imparted to us from our Father above.

It is so important to stand strong and not to allow the enemy to lie to us about our worth.

You have a very unique calling that only you can fulfill.

You can truly soar on the wings of love but if you look down you will immediately lose sight of the pinnacle that is set before you.

Look up and start to see as our Father sees.

The views above the storms of life provide a much better perspective than the viewpoints of attempting to look through the storms. This provides such a better clarity.

Let's all stop sinning. Every time we fall, we get burned. Thank goodness there is forgiveness available so that we can climb back on top.

Love continues with the following words of admonition:

> If ye abide in me, and my words abide in you, ye shall ask what ye will, and it shall be done unto you. Herein is my Father glorified, that ye bear much fruit; so shall ye be my disciples.
>
> John 15:7–8

All we have to do is ask, to reflect and apply His foundational truths.

> Study to shew thyself approved unto God, a
> workman that needeth not be ashamed, rightly
> dividing the word of truth.
>
> 11 Timothy 2:15

So how much does God love us?

Jesus clearly states, "As the Father hath loved me, so have I loved you: continue ye in my Love." (John 15:9)

Wow! Just think about the above verse for a moment. The same love our Father has for Jesus, He has for us.

We do have to realize that our Father is not always pleased with our actions. Any time we do what is contrary to Love by sinning, it hurts Him. Why? Because we are hurting ourselves and we break that sweet spirit of communion with our Creator.

It is so crucial that we be very quick to acknowledge our selfish actions and come clean. We can then partake of that living connection again that is so vital to us.

Jesus also said,

> If ye keep my commandments, ye shall abide
> in my love; even as I have kept my Father's
> commandments, and abide in his love. These
> things have I spoken unto you, that my joy
> might remain in you, and that your joy might
> be full.
>
> John 15:10–11

Oh, to be full of joy!

For this to take place, we need to truly understand that love precedes joy as is evidenced in the above two verses. Thus, we need to be full of His love if we ever expect to be full of His joy.

You might be asking, "Is this even possible?"

Jesus said "…The things which are impossible with men are possible with God." (Luke 18:27)

Obviously, the answer is yes!

How can we give something away if we have not first received it? But, when we do receive this awesome tranquility, we can't help but give it back to Him and to those we associate with.

This in turn brings such an indescribable joy that the world simply cannot offer.

The world attempts to offer a counterfeit with happiness which is based on temporary circumstances.

Let's look at a portion of Galatians 5:22 which states "But the fruit of the Spirit is love, joy, peace…"

The fruits of the Spirit are listed in a specific order as one leads into another. For now, I will just mention that love will always bring about joyous occasions which also yields His priceless peace.

Jesus declares,

> This is my commandment, That ye love one another, as I have loved you. Greater love

hath no man than this, that a man lay down his life for his friends. Ye are my friends, if ye do whatsoever I command you. Henceforth I call you not servants; for the servant knoweth not what his LORD doeth: but I have called you friends; for all things that I have heard of my Father I have made known unto you. Ye have not chosen me, but I have chosen you, and ordained you, that ye should go and bring forth fruit, and that your fruit should remain: that whatsoever ye shall ask of the Father in my name, he may give it you. These things I command you, that ye love one another.

John 15:12–17

It is such a high honor to be called a friend of Love.

As we can also see, Jesus is not holding anything back from us. Everything is available if we will put ourselves in a position to receive His glory.

There is so much to know from Love that we will still be learning throughout eternity.

Chapter 16

Every word that Jesus declares is for our benefit.

We tend to wander from His guidance, trip and fall and then ask why He has allowed certain events to take place in our lives.

Isn't it funny how we do the things we want to do and then get philosophical about the reasons why our dreams have not been fulfilled? Often, we think that it must not have been Love's will for us to be successful in a particular area if we do not see some of our hopes come to fruition.

Our Father will never do anything that would hurt us. We must fully realize Love is not going to force our hands to do anything we do not want to do.

He loves us so much that He has given us the gift of choice. What will we do when we hear His voice?

He will always lead you along the paths of victory. Let's be "…followers of them who through faith and patience inherit the promises." (Hebrews 6:12)

In Revelation 19:11 we see that "...Faithful and True..." is always with you.

If the world disappoints us, Love lifts us up to His glory to experience the ultimate levels of comfort and encouragement.

Now let's take a look at some of the reasons why the Holy Spirit has been sent to us.

In John 16:8–11, Jesus states,

> And when he is come, he will reprove the world of sin, and of righteousness, and of judgment: Of sin, because they believe not on me; Of righteousness, because I go to my Father, and ye see me no more; Of judgment, because the prince of this world is judged.

Jesus further states,

> Howbeit when he, the Spirit of truth, is come, he will guide you into all truth: for he shall not speak of himself; but whatsoever he shall hear, that shall he speak: and he will shew you things to come. He shall glorify me: for he shall receive of mine, and shall shew it unto you.
>
> John 16:13, 14

The Holy Spirit will make all things clear as truth always cuts through any fabrication.

Love is willing to reveal His glorious wisdom.

Are we in a position to ponder these wondrous workings? Allow Love to give birth to all of the beautiful plans He has designed for you.

Yes, there is pain at times as we live in a world that acts as if it is upside down.

Please believe me when I say that the greatest attacks always come before the greatest victories. I have witnessed this time and time again.

Allow His joy to flow within you and to refresh every dry area of your being.

Watch your circumstances change in a positive way like a delicate flower that gently unfolds to the light of day.

Ask for Love's best for you and be prepared to receive more than you can conceive. (See Ephesians 3:20.)

This all starts from within as "…the kingdom of God is within you." (Luke 17:21)

Let's look at some additional words of Jesus found in John 16:33:

> These things I have spoken unto you, that in me ye might have peace. In the world ye shall have tribulation: but be of good cheer; I have overcome the world.

Yes, it certainly is time to have peace in the midst of the storms of life.

Our setbacks are only temporary and soon we will be joining Jesus where all of the trials will cease to exist.

> Fight the good fight of faith, lay hold on eternal life, whereunto thou art also called, and hast professed a good profession before many witnesses.
>
> 1 Timothy 6:12

Let's keep in mind that love is still the ultimate foundation as "...faith...worketh by love." (Galatians 5:6)

Chapter 17

> These words spake Jesus, and lifted up his
> eyes to heaven, and said, Father, the hour is
> come; glorify thy Son, that thy Son also may
> glorify thee.
>
> John 17:1

Let's also bring glory to Love. How? By truly becoming
a family of unity in the Spirit.

We will cover this in detail as we further explore
Love's applications found throughout this wonderful
chapter.

> Jesus said, And this is life eternal, that they
> might know thee the only true God, and Jesus
> Christ, whom thou hast sent.
>
> John 17:3

Allow this verse to become one of many foundational verses for you as this is truly what life is all about.

Do you know Him or do you know of Him?

Do we truly know Love? If we do, we will also fully trust Him.

If you will study the New Testament, you will see that any of the individuals who turned this world right side up had a very intimate relationship with Jesus.

It's time for us to impact this world in a way that has yet to be seen.

Let's be a generation that is so touched with His compassion that we flow with a passion of purity to bring people into Love's eternal home.

Jesus also said "I have glorified thee on the earth: I have finished the work which thou gavest me to do." (John 17:4)

Let's also complete what Love has called us to do this day and that is to bring glory to Him.

Love and obedience are inseparable.

Jesus is the perfect example of both.

The more we receive from Him, the greater the responsibility we have to continue to walk in this light. What an excellent place to be in.

> But as it is written, Eye hath not seen, nor ear heard, neither have entered into the heart of man, the things which God hath prepared for

> them that love him. But God hath revealed
> them unto us by his Spirit: for the Spirit sear-
> cheth all things, yea, the deep things of God.
>
> 1 Corinthians 2:9–10

Let's start looking for "…the unsearchable riches of Christ." (Ephesians 3:8)

"In whom we have boldness and access with confidence by the faith of him." (Ephesians 3:12)

Love's eloquent words can also be found in Luke 12:32: "Fear not, little flock; for it is your Father's good pleasure to give you the kingdom."

Our Father's love transcends the highest heights. So let's look up, look within, for now is the time to receive from Him.

> For I have given unto them the words which
> thou gavest me; and they have received
> them, and have known surely that I came
> out from thee, and they have believed that
> thou didst send me.
>
> John 17:8

Will we do the same? If so, let's permit Love to fill us with His honesty so that there is no more room for any type of deception.

Our Father's sincerest desires are to protect us and to help us to walk in unity. (See John 17:11.)

If we walk with Love, we can quickly see that nothing "…shall be able to separate us from the love of God, which is in Christ Jesus our LORD." (Romans 8:39)

Jesus again mentions his willingness to protect us in John 17:15:

> I pray not that thou shouldest take them out of the world, but that thou shouldest keep them from the evil.

In all honesty, we take ourselves out of His protection whenever we commit a sin. This is another reason why it is imperative that we be quick to repent and quick to forgive.

You can look at Psalm 91 for a beautiful correlation of God's love and protection.

"Sanctify them through thy truth: thy word is truth." (John 17:17)

Jesus is clearly showing us that He truly wants us to be set aside for Him. One of Love's objectives is for us to fulfill His purposes and to stop blending in with the world.

> For my thoughts are not your thoughts, neither are your ways my ways, saith the LORD.

> For as the heavens are higher than the earth,
> so are my ways higher than your ways, and my
> thoughts than your thoughts.
>
> Isaiah 55:8–9

Let's start thinking right. Then, and only then, will we start acting right.

Let's also focus our sights on "…the Father of lights…" (James 1:16)

Certainly, the desire to do what is right comes from above.

Let's look at some of these benefits found in Psalm 37:3–6:

> Trust in the LORD, and do good; so shalt thou dwell in the land, and verily thou shalt be fed. Delight thyself also in the LORD: and he shall give thee the desires of thine heart. Commit thy way unto the LORD; trust also in him; and he shall bring it to pass. And he shall bring forth thy righteousness as the light, and thy judgment as the noonday.

What a fabulous declaration if we will just do what pleases Love.

> That they all may be one; as thou, Father, art in

me, and I in thee, that they also may be one in us: that the world may believe that thou hast sent me. And the glory which thou gavest me I have given them; that they may be one, even as we are one: I in them, and thou in me, that they may be made perfect in one; and that the world may know that thou hast sent me, and hast loved them, as thou hast loved me. Father, I will that they also, whom thou hast given me, be with me where I am; that they may behold my glory, which thou hast given me; for thou lovedst me before the foundation of the world. O righteous Father, the world hath not known thee: but I have known thee, and these have known that thou hast sent me. And I have declared unto them thy name, and will declare it: that the love wherewith thou hast loved me may be in them, and I in them.

John 17:21–26

It is extremely humbling to read these loving words of Jesus as it clearly demonstrates how much Love wants to be with us.

One with the Father, one with the Son, one with the Holy Spirit, it looks like we have truly won.

Chapter 18

As we look at the beginning of Chapter 18, we find the ultimate act of treason. (See John 18:1–6.)

We all have met people who have acted as traitors toward other individuals. It is inevitable as deceived people tend to mislead others.

It is time for us to stop doing anything that is contrary to Love's ways.

Why be like Judas when we can become more like Jesus? When we hurt one of God's creations, we invite the enemy into that particular facet of our lives.

There is no justification for our acts of disobedience. We need to quickly come to our Father and ask for His forgiveness and to stop any form of inappropriate behavior.

Let's stop thinking that we are better than others as we need to look at our own flaws and ask to be set free. (See Matthew 7:1–5.)

It is a common misconception to see ourselves as

being above another person's level. This is pride which entered into Adam after he willingly disobeyed Love. (See Genesis 3:12.)

It is so clear that we need to stop blaming our Father or others for our own poor decisions.

It certainly is "...a time to heal..." (Ecclesiastes 3:1) Let's allow Jesus to do the miraculous as it is all to His glory.

When we are more complete, we will then be in a position to "judge not according to the appearance, but judge righteous judgment." (John 7:24)

Looking at John 18:1–6, we also see that sin cannot stand in the presence of God.

In John 18:7–11, we see that Love freely laid His life down so that we can be free to walk in victory.

We look at the fact that Peter failed to acknowledge his association with Jesus. (See John 18:15–27.)

How many times have we done the same when we consider our very own actions?

As mentioned in Chapter 13, Peter became a better person. Let's follow the same paths of life and obedience.

Jesus said, "...Every one that is of the truth heareth my voice." (John 18:37)

Let's listen and glisten with His light.

When you truly find this tranquil treasure, words of life and wisdom will freely flow from within to help a world that truly needs significant direction.

Are we leading them up towards heaven?

> How beautiful upon the mountains are the
> feet of him that bringeth good tidings, that
> publisheth peace; that bringeth good tidings
> of good, that publisheth salvation; that saith
> unto Zion, Thy God reigneth!
>
> Isaiah 52:7

Chapter 19

None of us truly has an idea what Jesus went through just before and during the time spent on the cross.

Isaiah 52:14 gives us a clear depiction but how many of us have received a revelation of this barbaric brutality?

Let's read the words of this prophecy found in Isaiah:

> As many were astonied at thee; his visage was
> so marred more than any man, and his form
> more than the sons of men.

It was our lifestyles that brought Love to this point. He paid the price in full so we can freely receive this gracious gift of eternal life.

I pray that we all receive a revelation of the intense love that Jesus has for us. He was willing to die a horrible death and to be separated from His Father while He paid for our sins. (See Matthew 27:26–54.)

He was then raised to life so that we could also receive

this immeasurable gift that we can enjoy throughout eternity. (See Matthew 27:62–28:20.)

We all need to face the truth that it was for us that Love laid down His life, only to be made alive again so that we can also live with Him.

Let's die to ourselves by putting to death the desires of our flesh so that we can truly live a life of abundance on this earth.

Galatians 2:20 depicts this beautifully:

> I am crucified with Christ: nevertheless I live; yet not I, but Christ liveth in me: and the life which I now live in the flesh I live by the faith of the Son of God, who loved me, and gave himself for me.

I believe what this passage is also saying is that if you were the only one who would have accepted this truth, Jesus would still have endured the torment just to have you be with Him. This fact needs to become that personal.

I believe Love saw you while He hung on the cross.

You might be thinking, "I have lived a horrible life. Why would Love want me?"

Let's take a look at some of Luke's description of the crucifixion involving two criminals:

And one of the malefactors which were hanged railed on him, saying, If thou be Christ, save thyself and us. But the other answering rebuked him, saying, Dost not thou fear God, seeing thou art in the same condemnation? And we indeed justly; for we receive the due reward of our deeds: but this man hath done nothing amiss. And he said unto Jesus, LORD, remember me when thou comest into thy kingdom. And Jesus said unto him, Verily I say unto thee, to day shalt thou be with me in paradise.

Luke 23:39–43

Love is the ultimate act of forgiveness.

Let's also take a look at what Jesus said while lifted on the cross:

"…Father, forgive them; for they know not what they do…" (Luke 23:34)

Love said this while in excruciating pain and agony.

People made fun of Jesus and insulted Him, yet Love did not retaliate. (See Luke 23:35–37.)

Do we have any idea how patient our Father is with us? We hurt Him with our choices yet what does Love do with us?

Let's now take a look at 1 Corinthians 13:4–8:

> Charity suffereth long, and is kind; charity
> envieth not; charity vaunteth not itself, is not
> puffed up. Doth not behave itself unseemly,
> seeketh not her own, is not easily provoked,
> thinketh no evil; Rejoiceth not in iniquity,
> but rejoiceth in the truth; Beareth all things,
> believeth all things, hopeth all things, endureth
> all things. Charity never faileth…

If this is how Love treats us, shouldn't we show the same consideration?

It is not a matter of whether or not they deserve it, for we certainly did not deserve Love's ultimate sacrifice.

Jesus said,

> …If any man will come after me, let him
> deny himself, and take up his cross daily, and
> follow me.
>
> Luke 9:23

How is this done? By choosing to walk in love and forgiveness.

John knew the love of Jesus as we will see in John 19:26.

Let's actually take a look at John 19:26–27:

> When Jesus therefore saw his mother, and
> the disciple standing by, whom he loved, he

> saith unto his mother, Woman, behold thy
> son! Then saith he to the disciple, Behold thy
> mother! And from that hour that disciple took
> her unto his own home.

John received the utmost respect from Jesus as we see in the above referenced passage of Scripture. People can speculate about the meaning of the words Jesus spoke in this reference but I do not believe that anyone can discredit the amount of trust Jesus placed in John to carry out this commitment.

Are we truly willing to fulfill all that Love is calling us to do?

It is imperative that we stop being swept by the storms of life and to keep our eyes on the Captain of the helm.

> And the peace of God, which passeth all
> understanding, shall keep your hearts and
> minds through Christ Jesus.
>
> Philippians 4:7

As I pen the words to the end of this chapter, I lovingly want to remind you of all of the prophecies fulfilled in John 19.

The cross is Love's perfect plan so that we truly can

enjoy eternal fellowship with the Creator of all. Will you hold Him in awe?

Chapter 20

Much can happen in one day as we will see in this fascinating chapter.

Let's start with verse 1:

> The first day of the week cometh Mary Magdalene early, when it was dark, unto the sepulchre, and seeth the stone taken away from the sepulchre.

What "stones" are in our lives that have been hindering us from gaining entrance to our points of destination?

Are we willing to rise up before the light of day to seek our Father's presence?

It is so important for us to put Jesus first, this day and always.

Let's allow Love to purify us afresh each and every day. Okay?

We tend to get caught up in life's everyday activities and fail to look at the possibilities of a very personal interaction with the Creator of all miraculous events.

It is such a beautiful story of how Love appeared to Mary. (See John 20:11–17.)

Let's look at verse 17 a little more closely:

> Jesus saith unto her, Touch me not; for I am not yet ascended to my Father: but go to my brethren, and say unto them, I ascend unto my Father, and your Father; and to my God, and your God.

It is interesting to note that Love mentions the word "Father" before "God".

Yes, Jesus wants us to know first of all that we have a holy Father who lovingly looks after us and is always thinking of us.

If you will study the Word of God, you will begin to understand how much Love is interested in every detail of our lives.

Yes, Love is God, but first, He is our Father Who desires intimacy with us on the highest level.

There is such purity in this relationship that it defies

all logic. Love and holiness go hand in hand as you cannot separate the two.

Our lives should reflect living truths of both love and holiness. If we are not living in a way that is holy then we are not walking in Love's best.

I pray that we all begin to have a better understanding of what it means to live godly lives. To receive His love and holiness, to express this back to our loving Father and to extend these immeasurable gifts to those around us.

This world could be such a better place if we would take the time to understand what it truly means to be successful.

Will this be the day that we choose to obey?

It all starts with our thoughts.

> Casting down imaginations, and every high thing that exalteth itself against the knowledge of God, and bringing into captivity every thought to the obedience of Christ.
>
> 11 Corinthians 10:5

Let's begin to align our thinking with the concepts of His Word.

"But covet earnestly the best gifts: and yet shew I unto you a more excellent way." (1 Corinthians 12:31)

1 Corinthians 13 reveals that love is what life is all about.

Let's continue to be motivated to pursue what is exceptional which will help us to build enhanced relationships that can encompass the globe.

I will leave you with some following thoughts as we wrap up this chapter:

It is imperative we see that Jesus wants us to be full of "peace" as Love does not want us to be lacking in any capacity. (See John 20:19, 21, 26.)

Let's trust Him as He is more than capable of accomplishing all He has promised us.

Will we believe?

Chapter 21

As we look at the final chapter of this book, we find some fascinating information that is worth reflecting upon.

Jesus is always waiting for us to come to Him. Most of the time we are too busy doing what comes naturally as we follow the natural course of events dictated by the world. (See John 21:1–4.)

Love is so committed to us. It is a wonder why any of us doubt this glorious truth.

If you will look at John 21:5–13, you will see how Jesus always comes through with His abundant provision.

Sometimes, it appears our lives are empty. If we will continue to pursue His passions, we will eventually see that our lives can become full to the point that it even exceeds our highest expectations.

Of course, this all starts within. It will then transcend throughout our circumstances so that it will be evident to all who come in contact with us.

In John 21:15–17, we see Jesus giving Peter the outstanding opportunity of being redeemed from the three denials by confessing His love to Him in front of others:

> So when they had dined, Jesus saith to Simon Peter, Simon, son of Jonas, lovest thou me more than these? He saith unto him, Yea, LORD; thou knowest that I love thee. He saith unto him, Feed my lambs. He saith to him again the second time, Simon, son of Jonas, lovest thou me? He saith unto him, Yea, LORD; thou knowest that I love thee. He saith unto him, Feed my sheep. He saith unto him the third time, Simon, son of Jonas, lovest thou me? Peter was grieved because he said unto him the third time, Lovest thou me? And he said unto him, LORD, thou knowest all things; thou knowest that I love thee. Jesus saith unto him, Feed my sheep.

The cycle of defeat had now been officially broken so Peter could begin to glorify Love as we see in the Book of Acts.

Peter experienced a true life transformation which

is evident in his writings. (See the First and Second Epistles of Peter.)

I believe that John had a beautiful revelation of the love of Jesus. This is clearly portrayed in the Book of John as well as the First, Second and Third Epistles of John.

> And there are also many other things which Jesus did, the which, if they should be written every one, I suppose that even the world itself could not contain the books that should be written. Amen.
>
> John 21:25

Love has done so many wondrous things for us that we will need to wait to get to heaven to fully understand all of His wonderful works of compassion.

Let's continue to allow Love to create His beautiful works in and through each of us. It is all for His glory.

A Prayer of Salvation

If you would like to ask Jesus into your heart at this moment, I cordially invite you to say the following prayer:

> Dear Father,
>
> I do believe you sent your Son Jesus to provide me with eternal life. I also believe He died for me personally and was raised to life so that I can be with you throughout eternity.
>
> Jesus,
>
> I believe You shed Your precious blood and died on the cross so that I could truly be forgiven. I ask You to cleanse me from all of my sins and to make me new. Please come into my heart and give me a fresh start. I now believe I am one with You, this day and always! Amen.

If you opened up your heart to Love for the first time, welcome into the family that has been created from above.

Contact Info

If this book has been a blessing to you, please be advised that John Erol Kocer is available for speaking engagements. He can be contacted at johnkocer.com if you are interested in additional information. Thank you.